1/04

D0977677

above the line

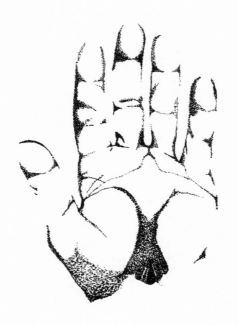

ABOVE THE LINE
New Poems

Joseph Bruchac

WEST END PRESS

Acknowledgments

Without small presses and literary magazines, and without the work
of dedicated anthologists, much of the best contemporary American
poetry of the past half century would never have been published.
Whatever success I have known as a poet has been due in large part
to the support I have enjoyed from hundreds of such publications,
some still with us, some held now only in the archive of memory.
I wish to thank them and the many dedicated editors it has been
my pleasure to know. I am especially grateful to the following
publications where earlier versions of some of the poems in this
collection first appeared:

Blueline for "Au Sable River Rapids" and "Thunder"
Crab Orchard Review for "Above the Line" and
    "Connecticut Shore"
The Manhattan Review for "Coyote's Car Wash"
Phati-tude for "Remembering Elms"
Rattle for "Red-tails in Flight"
Saratoga Poetry Zone 1998 Collection for "Geese," "Loon,"
    and "Kingfisher"

Hoofbeats, Claws and Rippled Fins: Creature Poems, edited
by Lee Bennett Hopkins, HarperCollins, 2002, for "Buffalo"

Home to Me: Poems Across America, selected by Lee Bennett Hopkins,
Orchard Books, 2002, for "Rez Kid"

*Seeing the Blue Between: Advice and Inspiration for Young
Poets*, compiled by Paul B. Janeczko, Candlewick Press, 2002,
for "Longhouse Song"

© 2003 by Joseph Bruchac
Printed in the United States of America

First edition, October 2003
ISBN: 0-9705344-8-5

Cover art: Chris Charlebois
Book and cover design: Nancy Woodard

West End Press • P.O. Box 27334 • Albuquerque, New Mexico 87125

Contents

811.54
BRY
2003

for Carol,
who makes it all possible

OHIO SITE

42 miles beyond Columbus
on 68 a house is burning
just to the west
of the four lane highway
near the town of Jeffersonville.

Seen from the air
it must be a bright
exclamation point
on this map whose makers
meant to tell no history.

The light of that fire
as it strobes the night
seems to my different
vision a throbbing heart
in a chest pried open
by the surgeon priest's
calm, white-gloved hands.

Two police cars parked
close to that blaze,
three men with torches
setting fire to a shed
make it clear
this burning
is just as sanctioned
as the bulldozers rumbling
to flatten the rubble,
making way for tomorrow.

Thick smoke
drifts back east
over the road,
swirled by the passage
of those who carry
with every turn of a metal wheel
the unforgiving violence
of that conflagration's bitter scent—
and I cannot stop crying.

But I've forgotten.
Perhaps you are not
one of our survivors,
one of those whose eyes
still remain stunned
by great walls of flame,
bitter blood and guns?
When you close your eyes
you cannot see
every cornfield and village
of the Shawnee,
every tree in the forest,
burning, burning, burning
and the cloaked sky weeping.

LONGHOUSE SONG

When I bend down to enter into the longhouse my sons and I made
this spring up in my grandfather's field, where the hooves of horses,
the sharp blades of plows and the throb of a tractor's heartless breath
once replaced an older way of seeing and staying close to the listening
land, it seems I can begin again, begin to hear this song:

Elm bark is my skin
bent saplings my bones
my mouth that draws
in the living wind
is the door to the coming of sun.

My breath
is the smoke
rising up to join sky.
My heart is the fire
in the circle of stones.

My eyes, my spirit
and my thoughts
belong to you,
whose human dreams
kept close to the earth
will always be held
in Creation's embrace
through the memoried
circles of seasons.

CLOUDS

No other century
until now
has seen the clouds
the way that we
have seen them
from on high.

But I do not mean
that we were the first
to lift ourselves into sky.

Thrust up by the roaring
throb of engines,
we watch clouds roll
under metal wings,
a skyscape white
as arctic lands,
unsolid shapes cut
into wisps of mist
as we descend
and shatter
floating islands
once imaged with angels.

But just because
we may purchase passage
on unowned wings
above that border,
that ancient blanket
spread across the sky
does not mean
we have learned
to understand
how a spirit can fly.

THE M'TEOULIN AND THE PRIEST

Once, they say, in a northern village
there was a Catholic priest
who tried to be friends
with an old Abenaki man
said to be m'teoulin.

That priest spent many
long hours trying
to convert his friend
to the right religion.

Then, one starless night
Songlismoniak,
the white men, came
into that little village,
bearded men in buckskin.
They were silent at first
then howled like those
whose hearts have been
frozen by the wind,
eyes empty of all
but death.

Some ran from them.
The French priest knelt
before his church.
"Close your eyes," he said,
Let us pray for protection."

The old m'teoulin
stood there.
To please his friend,
he knelt down, too.

The white men beat them senseless
with the butts of their longrifles.

They tied the two men
with rawhide thongs
and threw them back into
the church and then set it on fire.

When the priest woke up
smoke all around them,
he heard the old man chanting.

"Pray with me, now, brother,"
the m'teoulin said.
But the priest stayed silent
as the old man sang,
and sang and sang
sang with his eyes wide open.

Then the rawhide thongs
began to loosen,
they twisted like snakes
from their arms and legs
as the old man sang
and kept on singing.

Singing, singing,
he stood in the smoke,
lifted up the priest
carried him through the door
past the men standing guard.

It seemed as if
the old man's song
made them hard to see
as a small breeze
stirring the cedar trees.

By the bank of the river
the m'teoulin knelt
to treat the priest's wounds
with healing clay.

Then singing,
singing, singing, singing,
led him to a clearing
where other survivors
from the village were waiting.

They said they had heard
the old man's voice calling them
out of the darkness to safety.

"How did you do this?"
the priest asked his friend.

The m'teoulin smiled.
"Perhaps, brother," he said,
"You should try to pray once
with your eyes open."

ANSWER-
ING
MACHINE

With respect to Thich Nhat Hanh

Hello, I'm not here

Voices come from far away
This is my voice
It is not my voice
It is only words spoken
you mistook for me

Hello, at the sound you can leave

Let my words help
bring understanding
in this delicate dance
of electronic pulses
and countless heartbeats
of molecules and atoms
the discharge through cords
of recorded energy

Hello, I'm not there.
I'm not here,
I am here.

Even this message
is never the same.
It is the river that continues to flow.
This voice, my voice
is not my voice.

Did you remember
who you were
when you spoke?

You can leave,
you can leave,
you can never remain.

You can leave me
your message
it will not be your voice—

overlaid by the background
of voiceless voices
the whir of a fan,
the roar of a motor,
the hum of machines
that condition the air

and then, right there
in the midst of it all
as you paused,
did you hear behind you
the cry of a child
asking for attention?

Did you put down the phone?
Do you pick up the child,
did the crying cease?

Did the rumble
of engines continue forever?
Did the dry wind
keep blowing and blowing?

Or did you remember
at last where we are?
Did you find true compassion?

COMBING

Her hair gently,
adding more to the thousand
gossamer threads
of earth brown and silver
that cover her pillow
each morning now
as the full moon
still visible in the dawn sky
begins to measure
the start of another round,
the delicate piercing of the vein,
the flow through the syringe
of 5-FU, breaking the cycles
of quick growing cells.

The brush tugs
as roots release their grasp
like the feet of warblers
drawn by the pull of summer lands,
letting go of the highest branches
to begin long migration.

Her palm filled
with long strands of sacrifice,
she walks into the yard
to place her offering
upon the grass, so green
from the rain of the night
before that it seems to vibrate
in the living light.

Then she smiles,
thinking of the many nests
that will be interwoven,
the lives whose songs
will be embraced
by another loss
she has turned into a gift.

August 1998

PEKONGAN

*Pekongan is Abenaki for the block-end flute, a recorder-like instrument carved
from a spruce branch. The pekongan was traditionally used by a young man
who wished to win the heart of his future wife—who would then put words
to that song to make a lullaby for their first child.*

With breath borrowed from the wind,
the oldest circle will begin again.

A young man stands beneath the cedars.
Nanibonsad travels the starstrewn sky
as the trees listen, as the grasses listen,
as the insects listen, as the night birds listen,
as the animals listen, as the flowing streams listen,
and as the one within the lodge
waits to listen, listen to that first song.

He raises the flute carved from spruce
to his lips and gives it breath till
she comes from her lodge.
Her smile shows that his melody
touched her heart.
Her hand takes his hand
and the music continues.

Nanibonsad, the grandmother, crosses the skies
of night many times and now the hands
that made the flute finish a cradleboard,
bending the arch shaped like the rainbow,
inscribing the shapes of birds and trees,
grass and flowing streams.

Earth and Sky come together again
hands cupped to hold the little one.
As she sings the melody played
for her heart as she gives it words
to soothe their first child,
held peaceful and safe in the oldest circle,
this cycle of breath, love and song.

Nanibonsad: the Moon, literally "the Night Traveler."

DOGON VILLAGE

Tireli, Mali 1992

From the top of the scarp
the land fell away
baobabs and low brush
vanishing
into the old Sahara's grasp
of sand and stone,
while on the dry
breath of the wind
came the jingle
of a harness bell
as a Taureg rider
on his sleek camel
crested a distant horizon,
the dry smell of spice on the sun.

The village was nowhere to be seen,
only the reds, the browns, the grays
of earth, the circles and blocks of rock
until we looked again and saw
as our eyes took in
the subtle motions
of goats and people
at the foot of the cliff
that the town was there,
right there, a thousand feet below
blended so perfectly into all
that was around
and was within
that it was as open
and hidden to view
as every single grain of sand.

COYOTE'S CAR WASH

Let me tell you
again about Coyote,
what he did, that time
when those young women
at the Junior College
were having some kind
of a car wash to raise
money for some trip.

When he saw their sign,
that Coyote, he changed
himself into a red Ford Mustang,
a 78 with dirty mudflaps
and left himself parked in line.

Man, one of those
young women exclaimed,
this car is really, really dirty.
It just doesn't seem
to want to get clean.

This paint is so sticky
with bugs and gook
it feels like fur,
another one said.

So then they all
started working on it.

Hey, wait, did you all
hear the engine start running?
one of them called out,
her hands on the hood.
Wow, look at the way
it is dripping oil!

Coyote couldn't
contain how he felt—
he changed back into
his own scroungy self.

They chased him out
of there, dripping wet,
soaked with suds,
armorall aglisten
on his nails and teeth.

What kind of a story
is that? you say.
Don't blame me,
it's just Coyote's way.

GEESE

Before we see them,
we hear the geese
returning
from the distant south,
their calls
are like a pack of dogs
yelping over the clouds.

Onk-te-gwa, Onk-te-gwa
they call their name
as they circle the pond
before they glide
on grey wings,
wide spread
to slow their flight.

As they splash and surge
and bob in the water,
their voices are softer:
ghank-ghank ghank-ghank.

Then they lift their heads
to listen again
for the sounds of danger
or the voices of friends
brought to them
by their brother, the wind.

LOON

Comes flying in
on whistling wings,
its call in flight
a quick kwuk-kwuk-kwuk.

But when it is settled
down into the pond,
wearing its checkered
summer cloak,
it lifts its head
and yodels out
a trembling cry
that is like no other.

Hoo-ooo-ooo-ooo
and then it laughs
or wails in a voice
so high and sad
it might remind you
of the ancient story
of how the loons
lost their oldest friend
and thus their call
is a lonely longing for him.

At last it dives
and is lost to our sight,
gone into another world,
leaving only the haunting echo
of its music across bright water.

KINGFISHER

A rattling call across the pond
and then the flash of blue wings
up from the branch
of the old dead pine
that leans
out above the water.

With its necklace of white
it dips up and down
stitching its way over
the pond still
as a mirror
until
it cocks its head to hover
like a feathered helicopter
before it dives—
its beak an arrow.

The chunk of its splash,
and then the quick flutter
of its rising,
a shiner's tail
aflap in its beak
make ripples
across the morning.

THAW

When the ice
still covers
the pond's cloudy gaze
like the eyelids
of a sleeping giant,
it already is dreaming
the music of longer days.

Sun grows bright, then
ice shifts and breaks
into spiderwebs
and fantastic shapes
as if hands were pushing
up from below.
When you stand close
in late winter snow,
you hear the whispers
and groans as it wakes.

The thudding of
invisible feet,
the high warble
of a thrush's song,
even the rumbling drum
of distant thunder
flow out of the ice
in a breathless symphony—
the long year's music begun.

THUNDER

A deep growl
like a bear just waking
comes rumbling
not from earth, but above.
Then, like the sound
of heavy wheels
or a great boulder rolling
down an endless hill,
the thunder crosses the sky.

It sends a message
to the pond—
the moons of snow
are finally past,
the rains
will be returning now.

Open your mouth,
it is the time to drink
in this sweet season.

SIMMS LIBRARY
ALBUQUERQUE ACADEMY

RAIN

First silence
and then
almost like a sigh
the gentle
harp note plink
of a raindrop
that fell from so high
we can barely imagine
its sparkling journey
down
  from
     the
        sky.

It is the beginning,
the very first
note of a melody
older than breathing.

Long before we
who walk, swim or fly
arrived
this pond was singing.

WIND IN THE PINES

So soft at first,
just the hint
of sighing
then, as the boughs
and the long soft needles,
lend it a voice,
and the ripples spread
across the pond,
the wind starts to sing.

The pines quiver and bend,
moved by that long breath
that has flowed down the valleys,
lifted over the hills,
whistling, whispering
a chorus that fills
the air around us
as the whole forest
    bows and dances.

BLUE SPRUCES

I said farewell to the two blue spruce
my lumberjack grandfather planted
as seedlings fifty-five springs ago
when I was a small unsmiling shadow
always at his heel, reaching for his hand.

In that narrow strip of yard between
our former gas station's new garage
and the big house built up by my sister
around the frame of the old horse barn,
the trees had thrived, shooting up sixty feet,
just as I had grown to a greater height
than that man who was always my true north.

But now their seasonal cascades
of small sharp needles had grown too great
for roofs or gutters to continue to bear.
Crowded in by other trees around,
their branches were dying, their tops broken.
We could no longer leave them there.

We called in Paul, whose arborist hands
have planted far more than he has cut,
who speaks to each tree he must bring down
before he clips on the climbing strap,
before the roar of the chain saw starts.

All day the sound of the two cycle engine
came down from above like the steady cascade
of limbs shaped like the primary feathers
of birds as large as those in legends.
Below, the woodchipper's chest-rumbling growl
kept pace, as Vince fed in limb after limb,
spewing out a multi-colored gale to coat the snow
with ground bark and needles, xylem and phloem
and cambium layers tranformed into thick mulch.
The smell of the woods that I remembered
clinging to my grandfather's denim coat
when he came home from a long day's work
was everywhere in the pungent air.

This morning as I stand below
an emptiness of sudden sky
where I once looked up toward limbs as old
as earliest memory, I know there is now
one more pattern gone, one more missing part
of receding childhood, one more sheltering presence
I can no longer touch with a hand.

Yet the mulch from those limbs
will hold moisture, give strength
to the raspberry bushes below the stone wall,
add to each summer's sweet late harvest.
Rough planks milled from their trunks
will make solid bridges over Bell Brook,
be built into walls to give others shelter.

Just as spirit goes on
when flesh is no longer there.

AU SABLE RIVER RAPIDS

The man who stands, fly rod in hand
in the lower corner of the painting
is framed by the edge of a broken wall,
some once firm human foundation
flowing back to the contours of ancient stone.
The river that rushes, that flows downstream
like a deep breath always letting go,
cuts off the man from those distant figures
on the other side where the flow of water
is calmer, where trees may seem less wild,
where patient white walls of farm house and barns
speak of an order somehow controlled
even though the mountains, the dark green of forests,
always rise up behind and above all buildings.

The man looks back, perhaps eyeing a pool
where a lunker trout hides under the ripple,
but his knee is bent, the weight of his intent
will carry him out of this frame,
carry him upstream, at least for a time.

MOUNTAIN BURIAL

We dug the hole in the mountain soil,
thick mats of leaves and woven roots
resisting the shovel's sharpened edge
until a circle had been pried free,
exposing dark earth and five fist-sized stones,
one for each of his children
three sons, two daughters
who carried on the family line.

There on the southern facing slope
of the Kaydeross Range while a red-tailed hawk
whistled up a thermal high overhead
and the barking of geese carried through the wind,
where an ancient gray glacial erratic,
a boulder as round as a sweatlodge's shape,
was embraced by two trees, an ash and a maple,
we dug further down until the soil
turned iron red and the pulsing surge
of a hidden spring whose edge we had touched
brought a flow of water into the hole.

Daddy always loved the spring at the farm,
Carol says and then as we open the box,
pour out his ashes, ground white by the flame,
she smoothes them gently with her hand
then replaces those stones, stones for the living
and for one passed on, then another one
for her mother who chose this resting place.
Then we plant the rhododenron.

It is far from that room where those memories
that had sustained him almost nine decades
had begun to escape, walking away
in those final months; though he tried to follow
they became like shadows always
passing through the door before he could
call out one more time their names,
before, one morning, the light was simply gone.

Here on this ridge, just over the hill
from the place where my own grandfather was born,
here where the remains of more than one
of my own Indian ancestors lie hidden,
where a family gathers and stories are told
of a man whose love and pride for his family
holds generation after generation
as sun after sun returns and returns
his spirit is free, stories live in this wind,
bones feed old Abenaki roots
as a zembla red rhododendron's blossoms
echo a flame strong as love and blood,
an ancient warmth deeper than bone.

RED-TAILS IN FLIGHT

Two red-tailed hawks swirl overhead,
each circle finding a thermal's edge
to carry them higher, higher still
over the old Kayderosseras Range,
until their sun-narrowed shapes
become eyelash thin.

Yet as those hawks rise into sky,
their piercing calls dispel all distance.
With my eyes closed they are close, close, close. . . .

No closer than the throbbing drum
held within the chest, a grandparent's breath,
no closer than the centuried bones
hidden in these hills under maple and pine.
No closer than those whose shapes in dream
are neither man nor bird, but flight.

A hundred centuries spin away
as eyes rise high above our roads,
the metal lines of power strung
thinner than spiderwebs over the land.
Then vision widens as we lift our sight,
as that bone-thrilling call from the clouds
cuts through every distance of season or loss.

A man stands with his arms open,
relearning an ancestor's patient stance.
He breathes and swift as that indrawn breath,
he finds his fingers linked again
with the feathered hands of the wind.

WILD STRAWBERRIES

On the hill behind the old horse barn
wild strawberries glow like embers.
Many springs I looked to that place
to see the bending, bending shape
of a woman filling her basket
with Sun's first harvest.

It was my mother's favorite escape
to lose herself on a warm June day,
away from any human voices
that might hold anger or command,
demand attention to timebound things.
There, relations deeper than marriage
bound her again to a season of sharing,
sweet as it was when she was young.

An old Mohawk story tells of the boy
who helped the Djo-ge-oh, the Little People.
They took him to their secret caves,
gave him the gift of the first strawberries.
When he went home a whole generation
had lived and died and he found himself
a tall grown man returned to a place
that was both his own and strange.

Even after the wheelchair's embrace
tried to hold her away from the earth,
when she fell, sometimes as she lay there
her fingers moved on the hardwood floor
as if reaching for clusters of fruit.

In this second spring since she left breath,
I look to that hill, not knowing if
I am awake or deep in a dream,
yet knowing whose spirit I may see there,
picking the ancient heart-shaped berries
released from the heavy weight of flesh,
free to gather again, free to share.

REZ KID

The place we live isn't very big
compared to the land that once was ours.
This reservation we call home
is ten miles long by six miles wide.
And even though it's not that large,
the state cut a nice new four lane highway
right through the middle of the maple forest
where we used to hunt and get medicine plants.

My Grampa Bigtree has always had
what our people call a really well
developed Indian sense of humor.
He says it all worked out for the best.
It's made it a whole lot easier
for us to go hunting, although now it takes two—
one to stop the traffic while the other one
runs out to pick the game up from the road.
And even though he's only kidding,
he's showed me that if you know where to look
you really can find the old healing plants
growing next to that superhighway.

Sometimes tourists drive down the smaller road
that leads off the four-lane
then turns down onto Frog Street,
where the school and the church
and the box lacrosse field and the meeting house
are all crowded together.
Our Rez doesn't have a gambling casino,
our people have always voted against that.
So most of our houses and well-used trailers
look pretty old, in need of paint and some of them
have cars without wheels up on concrete blocks
parked in their front yards.
No one ever gets rich when they stay on the Rez.
If you live here, you have to share.

I don't think those tourists see what we see,
even though I always wave to them
when I'm out riding my old dirt bike.
They're looking for tipis and chiefs in headdresses,
not people who look pretty much like them,
not a dark-haired kid wearing sneakers and headphones
and nodding his head to Indian Rap.

Yeah, things seem different
than they did long ago.
Some of our own people
don't even know how to speak our language,
even though we teach it in our school.
Some leave the Rez and don't come back.
But some of us, like Grampa Bigtree,
know that hidden roots still give you strength.
There always will be another day.
The wind will always remember our name.
No matter how many roads they build,
the earth under our feet is our mother.

OLD BERRIES

Blueberries grow best in mountain soil.
Near the top of Algonquin Peak,
I filled a canteen with those small blue gifts
of sparse soil and thin rain and knife-edge sun.

These berry bushes are ancient here.
They came back to reclaim
after ice and fire these improbable heights.
Their roots wide spread
like dark fingers refusing to let go,
even though heavy feet and heedless steps
crush them against stone year after year.

A party of our people passed here
two short centuries before my breath,
heading north to the refuge, the deeper hills,
beyond the grasp and longrifle range of men
with eyes cold as the deadwater swamp,
gaze frozen on the chance of bounties
paid as quickly for Abenaki scalps
as for the skins of our brothers and sisters,
bear and wolf and mountain lion.

Here, a child's palms were held out
to cup berries picked by a weary mother,
strength found to walk a little further,
blue hope a promise of gentler times.

Here an ancestor lifted his palms
to give true thanks for another dawn
for the narrow path that still gives us survival,
for old berries holding hard.

BURIAL PLACES ALONG THE LONG RIVER

For John Moody

1.

I will not tell you how we know them,
those places along the river bank
where the wash and bend of Kwanitewk
will again reveal to the touch of sun
ancient bones of ancestors who were placed
beneath the sacred hands of fire.
Those places are where our villages were.

2.

One day, I canoed there with a friend
whose honest mind has not been twisted
by that strange disease the white men brought,
a sickness of the heart that they think
can only be cured by gold—men who,
as their ancestors hunted scalps,
now despoil our graves to sell pots and bones.

The river was thronged with other travelers
their motorboats eager to get them nowhere,
and like awkward eagles overhead,
a flight of ultralights whirred and snarled—
lawnmowers suburbanizing the sky.

3.

We turned into a quiet backwater.
There a great horned owl perched on a low limb.
Old ones, we said, we know you are here.
Then that spirit owl spread its wide wings
and floated, silent as a feather's fall
leading us back to a bank of blue clay, to a place
where the wind became a flute song,
where memory and vision were so intertwined
that for a time I forgot the name I carried
into this century and remembered more
than I had known before.

4.

I will not show you or tell you where,
where our spirits remain along the Long River,
so many of them upon both shores,
where the lift of flood still makes soil sweet
for the roots of corn, the sustainer of life.
Our old ones rest below our feet,
under the lodges where children dream
of a grandmother's voice, a grandfather's song
still heard in the night after breath was gone.
Our burials show where our villages are.

CEDAR FLUTE

Pekongan,
the cedar flute,
its hollow heart fills
with the flow of wind

Pekongan,
gift of the birds
long call of the loon
and the high hawk's cry

Pekongan,
a bright thread stretched
from one heart to the next
a sweet courting sigh

Pekongan
a touch beyond words
from the place past breath
where songs begin

FOUR

Four is the number
of Creation,
the four grandparents
who cradled our breath.

Four is the balance
of directions:
new dawn of east,
warm breath of south,
sunset red of west,
white-haired elder north.

Four is the connection
between the arms
of earth and sky,
the crossroad's logic,
unlike the triangle—
pyramid heirarchic
its sharp height elite,
while below the multitude
crushed by the weight
are unable to stand.

Four is the magic,
the choice made to share
our lives with
the ancient enduring ones,
Fire and Earth,
Water and Air.

COPAL, RED BLOOD

Chiapas, 1998

Copal incense, small figures molded
to sacrifice in the god pot's umbra.
A clearing at the rain forest's edge,
green and a thousand shades of green,
that same riot of verdancy that swallowed
Palenque and more stone-carved cities
than we have words to name.

Orchids, lianas, strangler figs,
philodendron, the buttressed roots
of mahogany and its sister trees
hold thin soil over honeycombed limestone,
hiding the entrances leading down
twisting into Xibalba, a snake's road,
where the hero Twins played ball
with Death and the Children of Death,
died, lost their heads, lived again and won.

Tall cane grass grows at the edge of a grove,
eight harvests after the corn gave way
to trees where fruits hang golden
as the faces of small glowing suns.
Arrow straight cane, arrowshafts pointing
up toward the many layers of Heaven,
the tongue of Creation's Creator.

Here, more than six centuries gone,
briared strings were drawn
through the willing tongues
of the nobly born, great ladies and lords,
offering their own blood from every mouth.

Divination, appeasement, and balance—
before the starving wars of invaders
who threw down the steles, burned the forest paths,
generations ahead of European hunger.

And then there was the second coming
that saw the pale armored shadow
of Quetzalcoatl cross the land.
Some say it was coincidence,
mistaken identity that gave
Hernan Cortez the old brother's name.
But that is not what the Lacandon know,
for that Rabbit Year was not dishonest.
The Conquistador was who he was,
a man so shrunken in memory
so forgetful of the gifts of blood
that now the taking of gold became
the only medicine that could touch
the disease of his shrunken heart,
a disease passed to all those descendents
who demand the people bow to them.
With American jets and machine pistols,
the ghost of Cortez marks his return.

And now, while copal incense burns,
the slow reach to the sacred goes on
long after each apocalypse.

Divination, appeasement, balance
remain before the end of the world,
while the Twins descend to play their game,
return when the world begins again.

FIRST SNOW IN NOVEMBER

When I see tracks
in the Freezing Moon
they make me want to follow.

The familiar green
of the grass is gone
and where there was a humdrum lawn
a map of white
the sky has placed
is filled with new trails to be traced.

The thump of
Rabbit's double print,
Old Fox's straight line trot a hint
of mysteries that have been sent,
a thousand stories evident—
right there outside my window.

It's time for me to go.

THE BODY OF THE LAND

How do we see,
shape our reflections?
How do we speak
when we give directions?

At the foot of that hill,
hued with the sun?
A headland here,
a body of water there?
Near the blue knee
of the river?

We cannot
find ourselves.

This true geography
of the land
escapes our
pale impersonations.

A bristle-back ridge
combs through the clouds,
whether seen or not
by images.

BUFFALO

Their great herds flowed
through the heart of this land
dark waters bursting from a dam.
Shaggy rivers of thunder rumbled down the plains
from Canada to Mexico and back again.
No one could guess their numbers then—
earth trembled under countless hooves,
dust of their passing darkened sun.

Even one bull buffalo, standing alone,
always turns its great head to face the storm.
Its muscles ripple with lazy strength.
Even the grizzlies, lords of the mountains,
turn away when Buffalo lowers his horns.

The old Plains nations praised Buffalo.
Lakota, Mandan, Cheyenne, Crow,
Kiowa, Pueblo, Arapaho
gave Buffalo thanks for giving them life.

Your meat is our food.
Your hide covers our tipis.
Your sinew strings our hunting bows.

They wept when the herds were wiped from the land
by the guns of white hunters, death-eyed men
who knew the red nations
could never be driven from their homes
while Buffalo gave strength to them.

Though fewer, the buffalo are not gone.
Here and there on wide park lands
you may see them graze among prairie flowers.
If you are quiet as you go
you may stand close, feel the ancient power
hear the hoofbeat song of Buffalo.

THE HAND OF BUDDHA
ON GEORGIA O'KEEFFE'S WALL

Abiquiu, New Mexico

The white bed
the open window
the dry earth
the cracked brown hills
the black door
the holy fingers
canvas, stretchers, hammer, tacks,
intensities of light.

"See what I see
outside the window. . .
earth pink and yellow
cliffs to the north—
the full pale moon
about to go down
in an early morning
lavender sky . . .
and a feeling
of much peace."

But where
have the Christian
Indians gone,
ceded this land
by Mexico
before General José
Marie Chávez
built this hacienda
of hungry ghosts?

Who was the one
who cut the hand
of Buddha from
another land
to nail it to
an adobe cross?

And why does this
whole story seem
as fragile as
an Eastern dream,
a pallete split
between so much
light and such deep
unspoken dark?

NEW HOPE FOR DEAD INDIANS

Late on a Sunday night,
almost Monday
not one week nor quite another
after watching the X-Files—
Indians caught in gravity warps
and Gila monsters head-imbedded
in stone—
and then listening
to a 1979 retrospective
on the radio with Dr. Demento,

a thought came
to me
as I drove toward
my cabin high on
the dark Kaydeross Range
rather like
a cloud approaching
a tree-covered ridge,
rising and then,
inspired by that height,
precipitating its moisture
in the form of healing rain.

It had, in part,
to do with Yoda,
whom I always think of as
spiritual child of
the Dalai Lama and
Yogi Berra,
his part played now
by a younger Muppets puppet
since the latest Star Wars
Sequel is a Prequel.

For, I have noted,
of late, in the movies
older actors are being portrayed
as children by their own children.

Except this is not a recent phenomena—
our offspring
bouncing back,
becoming ourselves
or even our own elders
from many generations before.

Who better to play
the very old
than the very young,
who better to be us
rewritten, rescripted, neater,
better than we were before
and not just in the movies
or on TV, but, as they say,
in life, in life, real life.

And I recall that time
in Calumet, Oklahoma
when the giant Cheyenne warrior
Stone Calf, who fought in the war
to save the buffalo,
appeared before me
in the denimed guise
of his great-grandchild.

And so I decided
to call this poem
New Hope for Dead Indians,
even writing these last lines
before the main body
of this text appeared
like a Moebius strip,
because
I really believe it.

PROPOSITION 666

All languages
are beautiful?
Is that
what they say?

How absurd. Next thing
those people will try
to prove is that
all gods
are beautiful, too.

But only we
know what is true,
that our god,
our tongue
is the only one,

the only one
our real nation reveres
especially when
our god of grace
is strangling
one of theirs.

NAGUALITO

You must understand
that to be seen
as a crow

is to
be viewed

as one
with wings

as one
who can
choose to fly.

ABOVE THE LINE

Jesse's face stayed dark
despite Northern winters.
So he never went
with us again
on those long migrations,
taken each Easter,
as we drove down
old military roads
Louis Bowman marched
into the South.

Plank trails bordered
by banks of roses
rising mist like smoke
and smoke like mist
eight decades and
two lifetimes gone.

Did my Indian Grampa
remember
his own father's
resurrection?

Four days left for dead
on the wilderness field,
while Thunder beings
rumbled an older chant
than Abenaki drums,
he drank the gift
of rain to survive,
that one who lived
to be my great-grandfather.

So many years
that I did not see,
as I walked
without knowing
above that line.

For though we paused
at Gettysburg,
to my eyes of eight winters
it was only another
glue-eyed attraction,
no more than a roadside
reptile farm
where rattlesnakes struck
at the panes of tapped cases,
pale fingers safe
from defiant coils,
segregated
by yellow-venomed glass.

Even though
we always drove on deeper
into the heart
of Old Virginia
to the healing springs
of Algonquin stories,
neatly held now
by a century
of resort spa walls
keeping out older dreams
as white-gloved waiters
with mahogany faces
carried trays of food
polished so bright
that the silver became
a mirror clear enough
to reflect the pain
of partial freedom,
I think somewhere

in the back of my mind
I only heard a cartoon bluebird
perched on the shoulders
of old Uncle Remus
beaming a smile so broad
and shallow that it hurt his face
as they sang
a Song of the South.

My grandfather only
went once with us
to visit those places
of his wife's relations.
He could barely read,
but he'd read enough.
The sign on the wall
in a roadside station
was spelled out to him
in large black letters
nothing less
than WHITE.

Those stains of skin
and scarred generations
never overcame an old knowledge
of remembered waters and healing darkness.
His silence stayed like
a slow river flowing
until it filled my own
innocent heart,
his wordless refusal taught me
the way our old people
always have known, that
our arms can be raised
to resist or embrace.

BLESSING THE WATERS

There is no blessing older
than the blessing of the waters.
It is in the flow of birth
and the joining of streams.
It is after the end
and before the beginning.
It is the circle
which owns no beginning or end.

As we walk beside the waters
we bless the waters
and they bless us in turn.

As we walk beside the waters,
we carry the rivers within us.
We are rivers walking
we are streams dancing.
We are the oceans
and the deserts joining hands.
We are the clouds and the rain.

As we thank the waters,
the sacred flow of life within us
is blessed by the winds of breath
by words and prayers
moist with the sweetness of water.

As we touch the waters,
as we lift the water to our lips,
as we pour the water over our bodies
as we greet the waters
as we thank the waters
we are equal in blessing
we are equally blessed.

In the flow of tears
in the flow of blood
in the flow of songs
we touch that which is sacred
as only water can be sacred,
for without water
there is neither life
nor the possibility of life.

So, once again
and once again,
we lift our hands to bless the water
knowing it is blessed without our blessing,
knowing it is blessed within our blessing,
and our songs are the surge
of the always returning tide.

LONG RUNNER

For John Worthen
(1944–1998)

Because he was
always so much in love
with even the smallest
gifts life could give,
one note of music from a guitar,
a voice sharing familiar tears
or laughter over the telephone,
the flight of a single distant bird
above the misty river at dawn,
the delicate tremble of her skin
felt even by a weakened touch,
so little for others
for him was enough.

That smile would always
come fleeting back
like sun after the clouds' dark chill.
Even when the body's traitor cells
stretched him, relentless, on the rack,
he would stand again, keep limping on,
less for himself than from his need
to share with us the stubborn hope
of his private Marathon.

He carried his message
far beyond the borders
most bodies or hearts could stand,
crossing one finish line after another,
his passion like a healing charm,
held up by an unbending will,
believing in a second wind
defying even the thoughts
of dying until he fell,
short of our arms.

But now, as his ashes
swirl to embrace
the river's flow
and the throb of ocean,
his pace has changed,
but is sure in its rhythm.

All the memories
of his athlete's breath
are freed at last of pain.
Whole as the wind, as wide and sure
as the ancient, shining road of stars,
his spirit is running again.

DOGON RELATIONS

Mali, West Africa

From the top
of the Bandiagara escarpment,
millenia of stone upthrust over Sahara,
the village below could hardly be seen,
the flow of stone and soil the same
as that of each house's symmetry,
each unpaved lane a tributary
flowing into the ancient desert
and the bush that throbbed
like a drum in the sun.

As seen on the Discovery Channel,
Ancient Mysteries or Terra X,
an awed Nimoyan voice's whisper
would have us subscribe to such beliefs
as that these people in this Dogon village
are but the sadly denatured descendents
of a powerful and unearthly past,
a fountaining time of ancient starleapers,
the deep knowledge of invisible galaxies
held in the design of a millet-filled granary:
"its shape exactly that of a spacecraft!"

I've heard it before,
such sweet pseudoscience
linked to prehistories
of my own Old People—
glacial scratches
turned to Ogum script,
sadly confused nomadic tribes
stumbling over the Bering landbridge
in search of mammoths,
late-comers, all.

Or do you remember
the last century's claim
that we were, in truth,
Israel's Lost Tribe?
Or, even better,
that we were typed
as supporting actors
in that cast of thousands,
that Mormon pageant,
dead serious, now,
when Jesus Christ
came to our New World
to stage a second passion play
for us Indians, yeah, Indians.

Let us not go there,
but back to the village of Tireli
where the elders, Muninyu and Asama,
shook our hands with warmth
as the fox diviner incised shapes in sand
and the desert fennec placed footprints there
that told us our coming
was expected and welcomed.

On the day that we left, I took out the sage
I'd brought from another distant desert.
We know that, they said,
we have that here, too.
Our ancestors were relatives.

I touched it to fire
and the incense smell
was carried on the sahel wind,
as they bowed their heads,
cupped their fingers to scoop
cleansing smoke to their hearts,
a blessing we shared.

CONNECTICUT SHORE

For my Mohegan relatives

Pale hands of starfish
hold firm against
the repeated rush
and rumble of waves
as the swell of tide surge
flows rockweed tresses
below the dipping wings of gulls
soaring, then dropping,
their sharp beaks keen
to the tremble
of surface-skimming shoals.

We stand, measuring
the river's end
by looks, not miles
from Wonbi Wadzoak,
the tall white mountain
at the start of the sky trail
the road up into our stars.

Our languages are remembered here
by the shapes of stone
whose true names embrace
Algonquin words
that sank beneath
the measured weight
yet remain undrowned
by imperial English.

Kik ta spemkik, ktsi wliwini.
Earth and sky, great thanks
I stir fire sand—
ashes to wind, wind to waves—
while hands of starfish
calm below the surface
hold hard against the rush of history.
The tide flow deep
in the chambered heart
remains a drum, pakholigan,
filling, strong with the memory of sea.

TIME ZONE

For Carol

Your exhausted voice
from our far away hill
weeps over the phone
after one more round
of that sickness so deep
it throbs like a spike
driven into a rib bone.
Yet another day of that aftermath,
inexorable as your body's rough grief
for those cells, unwanted and wanted both,
that now release their grip on life.

The helpful poison
flushes its way through seas
of pale corpuscles, tiny hearts,
wings fluttering, flags for
some sort of surrender.

But how can I speak such poetry
over this distance?
I can only say
I'll soon be on my way
back home—that word
we love and suffer for.

This evening we need
no miracles more
than the passing of
one endless night,
the melding of two zones of time,
the grace of another sunrise together.

THOSE CHEROKEE

Knew some things we didn't.
To us, north of their warmer lands,
Moon was an old woman
grandmother-wise, her eyes filled
with a warming light, yet wise
enough to leave heavenly space
for darkness and the stars.

Sun, the bolder elder brother,
was the one who loved
to watch men sweat
or even bleed and so
we offered him stick ball games
and war. . . .

Those Cherokee saw it
another way.
Sun was a woman,
her eyes always open
to the things we humans
do on this land.
Moon, her brother,
was dimmed by her light,
his own a pale reflection.

SELLING MANHATTANS

A drink, not history,
equal parts of alcohol,
deliberately crafted deceptions
and blood thick as Vermouth.

Near Wall Street, a barrier
made of wood and dreams,
made strong enough
to keep out us northern Mahicans,
sixty guilders is still sufficient
to buy an island
worth its weight
in trade goods.

Shaken or stirred
it's the same hangover,
a morning after
where even the birds
who once loaned their names
to a people of songs
must look hard
most mornings
to make out
the dawn through
Con Ed–addicted smoke.
Wooden high heeled shoes,
stiletto red,
rusty loaded cannons,
the mingled bones
of Peter Minuit
and Lenape sachems
whose names lie buried with them,
turn up as briefly
as American memories
in excavations
where the footing is poured
in thickening concrete
meant to hold down
as much
as it holds up.

REMEMBERING ELMS

Those great trees once lined every street
until, in times our children
cannot remember, all the elms began dying.
They were hit hard by a Dutch disease
winged from stand to yellowing stand
by small whirring beetles boring in death
their tunnels marked under shedding bark
like hieroglyphs—each skeletal tree a book of the dead.

My own heart fell with every tall tree.
I felt the emptiness, a landscape lost
like my Indian people stripped of a history
older than any discerned by those
who raked up raked the sawdust
from shadeless lawns.

Before the tall ships brought new diseases,
we were many and rich with elms,
the songs of their shade a lullaby
stolen from this grieving land.

Yet, decades later, small elm saplings sprout
each spring from hedgerows
and here and there, like whispers in the dusk,
deep in our forests a few tall elms still stand.

No longer young, I place my hands
on their rough bark and pray this promise—
that some of us, more than a few
and never the last of our kind,
will always stand with them.

LONE COYOTE

The man with the headband
who delivered the planks
to repair our deck,
I'd seen him before
at the lumberyard.
That flair, almost
an elegance in the way
he undoes the canvas straps
and flips them back
over the flatbed,
reminds me of how
I watched him draw
the circular saw
halving two-by-twelves.

The same bone choker
of a wingspread eagle
is around his neck
and so, this time,
instead of just saying
it with our eyes
I ask him the question.

In answer he tells me his tribe:
Mescalero Apache.

His hair is white
with early snow,
his face, like mine,
maps through the years
of half a century or more
of our own lifetimes
plus those crossing trails
of trade with Europe
and I believe him.

He lives, he says,
on Lake Desolation,
up there on the mountain,
pointing with his chin
just a ridge away
from this ridge
hawks cross
with as much ease
as his hand fans out
to gently grasp mine
as we give each other
our names.

LEAVING

Already almost too late to leave,
my son off to one state and me to another
and both of us deep in the state of confusion,
phones ringing, and usually welcome friends
unexpectedly knocking on our door,
our dog vomiting on the rug,
the furnace in the old house coughing,
then breaking down for one final time.
We struggle suitcases out the door, put my bag
into his backseat, not mine, then he roars off
in his Ford Expedition.

My heart is clenched like a boxer's fist,
my head feels as if this ultimate turn
of a crazy day's vise will make it pop
like a cantelope under a tractor tread.
Already almost too late to leave,
my luggage gone with my dutiful son
and the airport still forty miles away.

All of my own father's familiar anger,
all of those old unforgiven phrases
threaten to fill my mouth with bile.
I push them away before my face
grows as red as my shirt.
Slow down, slow down.

I am on that plane now, left behind
are books and catalogs, audio tapes
and all my new folded underwear.
In flight, on my way, I begin to recall
so many other hurried departures,
some of them too early and all of them
much easier than we ever expected.
As earth falls away, I must remember
how little it is that we ever take with us,
how soon we all will be on our way.